I0154263

One Disturbed Mind,

To Another

by L. D. Sowl

Someone may have stolen your dream when it was young and fresh and you were innocent. Anger is natural. Grief is appropriate. Healing is mandatory. Restoration is possible.

~Jane Rubietta

One Disturbed Mind, To Another

By L. D. Sowl

Copyright © 2011

All rights reserved.

Printed in the United States of America. No part of this book may be used or reproduced in any manner whatsoever without written permission except in the case of brief quotations embodied in critical articles and reviews.

All people and facts in this book are fictions. Any resemblance to real people or facts is coincidental.

Fifth Estate Publishers,

Post Office Box 116, Blountsville, AL 35031.

Cover art by Angela E. Stevens

Printed on acid-free paper

Library of Congress Control No: 2011931156

ISBN: 9781936533121

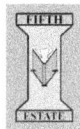

Fifth Estate

2011

Forward

These writings were produced over the last two years of my life. Some come from a place of deep grief, others come from a place of recognizing where God is in the midst of all our trials.

I was married 21 years to a man who became very sick with Bipolar Disorder over the years and who became increasingly verbally violent and environmentally violent towards me and my children. The depth of which is fodder for another book at another time.

It turned out the he had led a double life most of our marriage and the children and I had to get protection from the courts as I proceeded to divorce him.

It was through these many trials and sufferings that I found release in creating word pictures of how I felt that I could somehow feel relief from the pain and the guilt.

I have shared a very few of these writings with dear friends and they encouraged me to publish because they said they were touched. Many are intensely personal and have great meaning to me, but I have found that they also had great meaning to others.

It is my hope that by publishing this very personal and painful emotional journey that I have been on, that others will realize they are not alone and that someone else has felt what they have felt.

I have endured heart break from the men who tried to show up in our lives but I learned to love again even though I got my heart broken. At least that part still works in my heart. For that I am grateful.

I am including a picture showing how God spared me and loved me through some of this.

My last encounter with my ex-husband resulted in him trying to hit me with this push broom. He swung it five times and missed every time. If you look closely you can see how it is bent and the broom part shattered into two pieces.

These poems are about survival, hope and learning to love again. Reaching out and not being afraid to get your heart broke again until you find the friends and the love you were meant to have in your life. To not be afraid to reach for those things, yet again.

One of the many things my children and I have also learned is just how many people are available to truly love on you and help you and that there are just as many people out there ready to take advantage of you and your vulnerability.

Our list of thanks is long and if I forgot anyone please forgive me: Angela Stevens, my sister in all ways; Kim White, you keep me lifted up; Joseph Lumpkin, you believed in me and guided me out of stupidness more than once; Ashland Brethren in Christ Church for feeding us and praying for us; Glenna Amiralian for always being there; Amy Stephenson, my sounding board; my parents for making sure we had a place to live; my brother for kicking my butt regularly; my sister-in-law who coached me on my way to my new job; my martial arts students who brought joy to my life in class; and my children who are so resilient and my joy.

Table of Contents

Battered Flower

Long ago

I was a seed planted in love

I was fed and watered

Cared for in the sunshine of that love

Gentleness brought forth my beauty

Serene, like the flight of a dove

My stem was so slender, green and strong

My petals, soft and bright

I was well tended in my soil

Beauty and love were all I knew

Love came easy, without toil

Time came

I was uprooted from my father's garden

Repotted into another's soil

He was trusted to love and take care

To foster the beauty that attracted him

And at first, love was there

But then

I stretched out my leaves

To reach for the sunshine of love

I sunk my roots for nourishment

I thirsted for the water that gives life

But instead received batterment

Neglected

Given just enough to survive

My stem weakened, my petals dulled

My roots curled inward without love

Shielded from the warm love of the sun

Beauty faded, I weakened without that promised love

The gardener

He left me alone, to tend to myself

Dried and brittle, starving, dying

A plant that had almost no life

In a pot that had nothing that I needed

But I was glad for the end of strife

So long alone

I had forgotten what love was like

I felt dead inside, and had almost no life

Who would want a plant such as me?

A faded flower, broke with need

It seemed over, but then came he

With gentleness

He gave my parched roots water

He nourished my brittle body

He stroked my petals and spoke soft words

Put me in the warm sunshine

Tended to me as a shepherd does his herds

Very slowly

My weakened stem started to green

Under his love, my roots again took hold

My dried, faded petals began to return

Sweet nectar again filled me

Beauty within began to burn

Butterflies came

To rest on my new found form

Honey bees drawn once again

Sunshine and warmth and love

Were what he brought me to live

His care was a rare gift from above

Although

Older and wiser and damaged

My true form re-emerged in full bloom

Happiness and joy that I once knew

Long ago when I first grew

Have returned because of you

Secret Love

Love in secret is most wondrous and true,

You loving me, me loving you

Stolen time together is heavenly bliss,

I can still remember our first kiss

Loving without bound or restrictions

Free from all expectations

In the course of time all we really knew

Is you loving me, me loving you

Some would call it wrong, and they would be right

But the heart wants what it wants against our might

Tender words, embraces, kisses and passion abound

In this love that we have found

Joy and happiness are found by just a few

And I'm ok with what all we do

Because after all it is only just

You loving me and me loving you

The Lord is a Gentleman

He is a gentleman

He never intrudes

He stands in the shadows

Waits for me to choose

His love is like roses

Whose bloom never fades

He covers me with care

And expects nothing

He's with me when I rise

He's with me at night

His love draws me closer

Because it is quiet

He calls to me softly

Beckons me with words

Too wonderful to hear

Always what I need

In the time I need most

His love is complete

And I need nothing more

<u>Alone</u>

Yet all these people stand with me

I am still alone

The decisions are mine to make but

I make them alone

The more who come beside me

The more I feel alone

The devil speaks his madness

While I am alone

God sends His peace, His comfort

When I am alone

My soul is crushed within me

I am so alone

Deciding what is right and wrong

While I am all alone

Fearing what I'll lose if I ride the wave

I fear it all alone

Knowing if I don't react

I really will be all alone

Stand beside me one last time

So I am not alone

Let me breathe your courage in

So I can stand one last time, alone

There is Nothing

There is nothing so sweet

As hearing my name

Breathed from your lips

There is nothing so beautiful

As seeing love reflected

Back to me in your eyes

There is nothing so amazing

As the feel of your body

Shuddering in pleasure with mine

There is nothing so painful

As being separated from you

For any length of time

There is nothing so freeing

As being able to be me

Without fear you will leave

There is nothing so branded

As my heart and my mind

With the visions I have of you

There is nothing so perfect

As your face and your body

For they inspire me

There is nothing so wondrous

As knowing you choose me

To be a small part of your life

Fight

My heart beats fast within my breast

Even in the stillness, there is no rest

Fear rides the crashing wave as it crests

Tangling my nerves together as lofty sparrows' nests

Even the knowing of how much I'm blessed

Doesn't bring the elusive, much needed rest

I can feel the beast snaking through my chest

Tentacles probing my mind as if to test

The place where its damage will be done best

I must fight to win, to shed this pain lest

I lose myself forever to its celebratory fest

Waiting

I waited for him quietly

Impatiently and full of anxiety

Stillness in the mountain air

Soon my lover would be with me there!

Hearts and soul, already merged

Anticipation of the night through my body surged

When, O when, did I allow my heart to trust and love again?

When did I allow this attachment to begin?

Acceptance of the here and now

When my heart? and how?

Soon, very soon, the key will turn in the door

And my lover will make me his forever

Taking what has grown inside our hearts and minds

Making it a physical bond that binds

He is here now! My heart has leapt into my throat!

Here in the mountainous region so remote

My eyes drink him in, my lips find his

And all is well and I realize, this is what it is

It is all we can have, it is all there will ever be

Stolen moments in time, for my lover and me

Invisible chains keep my heart locked to his

Now all my body will know is him and this

Left behind and alone, my heart aches for my lover

The one who has captured my heart, my mind

And my body like no other

Photo by Leslie Sowl

You

Your skin is warm

Like sand on the shore

Your scent as fine

As red Summer wine

Salty streaks and strands

Grace hair once so dark

Your lips upturned in a smile

Beckons me stay a while

Your eyes call me close

As your hand takes mine

My heart begins to race

When sweetly we embrace

Your words spoken softly

Caress my ears with their tone

Bodies fit together

Hearts knit forever

Stained

The sky is blackest at midnight

No stars to light my way

Vapors closing in around me

Exhaustion causes me to sway

I feel the sand between my toes

It's shifting, sucking pull

As the waters edge laps at me

My mind with fear is full

The wind whips and snaps my hair

It tears and rents my clothes

Sea spray and rain sting my skin

The pain of all my woes

Not a single soul is near for miles

No help is coming for me

As I fight just to stand in the storm

And not be dragged out to sea

As I choke back tears

And try to breathe

And stand strong a little more

I realize I can because I believe

And it removes the fear

<u>Confused</u>

Through love and lust we wander lost

Though friend or foe, we never know

Each day brings forth new things to see

But wandering still, confused are we

Truth be known to those who seek

The lost, the found, the humble, the meek

And love, it comes to those who wait

Like strangers arriving at the gate

Our time is short, happiness shorter still

Work to be done and fields to till

Harvests to gather and children to rear

But I wait for you, Lord, to come near

Days Ahead

It was dark and heavy

My days were crazy and filled

Many times I didn't know what to do

And then God brought me you

Very little of the sun

Ever broke through my heart

That place where passion grew

But then God brought me you

The time was short

And the happiness was brief

But I learned my heart was open

And that God would bring me though

Days ahead without you

The Man You Long To Be

There's more to you

Than most can see

There's depth to you

That longs to be free

Beneath anger and pain

That inner rain

Is the man you long to be

The Way I Feel About You

I don't know what it is that makes me feel this way

I think about sitting with you late into the night on the porch swing talking

I think about watching movies with you snuggled up on the couch

I want to drink coffee with you in the morning before the day starts

I want to sit next to you in church

I want to wake up in the middle of the night and feel you next to me

I want to jump into your arms when I see you, and I have visions of running to do the same when you come home from work

I love the way your mouth tastes

I love the scent of your skin, even when you have been working

I need to feel your hands on me and your lips greedily on mine

I don't have to sleep with you to know how sex would be, I just know

It seems like forever when I don't see you, or hear the sound of your voice

I want to feel the soft feel of your fingers entwined with mine

I like the way your hair feels when I put my fingers in

it

I feel safe when you hug me close

Every night I spend away from you hurts me inside

When I don't hear from you it cuts me in ways I can't explain

I don't know what all this means, I just know how I feel

And I see your eyes, all the time

It doesn't matter if you feel the same,

I don't expect that you will

But for the time I have with you

I will take what I can and enjoy you

And if you ever feel the same, then I think we'd be the happiest people I know

Because short of being with my kids, I'm happiest when I am with you

I want to do everything with you

I don't care who knows how I feel

It only matters if you are ok with it

I don't know what this is that makes me feel this way, but I am thankful because it makes me feel alive

Wasn't Really Mine

I am thankful for you

For time that we had

For laughs that we shared

For passion you awakened

Although the pain of losing

What I never really had

But felt so deep inside

Cuts me through and through

I will never be sorry

And I am thankful to you

Missing

I miss the sound of your voice

I miss the taste of your kiss

I miss the feel of your hands

I miss the smell of your skin

And in the end

I miss what could have been

Forever

I see forever in your eyes

I don't need flowers

I don't need cards

Because I see forever in your eyes

I don't need jewels

Or fancy things

Just that promise of forever in your eyes

The feel of your lips

The touch of your hands

And the fire of forever in your eyes

<u>Joyous</u>

My heart is full of joy

There is lightness in my step

You've made it so I can't retreat

Into the darkness where I once planted my feet

Through fire and trials

You've grown my faith

Through love and through your word

I have come to where I should

<u>Blue</u>

The sky is blue

Its colors amazing

The ocean, too

Many shades of blue

No variation I've seen

No shade or hue

Are as amazing as your eyes

And that particular blue

<u>Snake</u>

The snake coiled gently, smoothly, quietly around my body

He is working his way up to my neck

He is warm and the hugging pressure,

I welcome it

I feel *some* thing, he makes me feel before the last goodnight

The snake is in love with me for now

I will be his meal after my last breath

I welcome the darkness, the being useful to him

It is hard to breathe, but I don't fight it

All my fight is gone, my strength sapped

I can feel the darkness coming now

The air has stopped flowing to my lungs

I am grateful to the snake as my death shall be painless

The light is dimming, it means no more pain, rejection, or suffering

I see my children's faces one at a time and I bless them in my mind

The darkness is here and I remember no more

And thank my God for this rest

Empty Space

There is a space that's empty

My heart is hollow there

It's not the place where God dwells

It's the spot that he held

In the waiting

You perfect my faith

In the darkness You make me wait

My fear begins to rise

It starts to clog my soul

But You give me song

And make me whole

You who hardens hearts of men

Who subvert justice in chambers for your people

Won't you also soften hearts

For the uniting in love of Your people?

Hardest at Night

When I am alone in the night

It's the hardest for me

I can feel your arms pull me tight

And then begins the imagery

The taste of your lips

The smell of your skin

The feel of your hips

As we move together again and again

Stomach to stomach

Thigh to thigh

The feel of you in me

When we are locked eye to eye

It's hardest at night

When I am alone

Crawling

My skin is crawling

It feels like its peeling away

I wish that this feeling

Would just go away

A hundred showers

And the strongest soap I can find

Won't get rid of

This awful grime

It's from the inside out

All this dirt that I feel

Contamination so deep

And horror so unreal

He Is There

In the middle of my deepest sin

He is there

In the middle of my darkest hour

He is there

In the middle of my loneliest times

He is there

In the middle of my greatest pain

He is there

In the middle of every time in my life

He is there

I am never alone, even when I feel that way

Because He is there

When everyone else fails me

I can trust the one who died for me

Because He is there

Yearning

Yearning, yearning

All the time yearning

Fearing, fearing

All the time fearing

Helpless, hopeless

All the time drowning

Worthless, ugly

Always feeling unlovely

Constricting, binding

All the while struggling

To believe

To hope

To dare

To trust

To love, yet again

Tape

It plays day and night

This tape in my head

It saps all my fight

Keeps me from rest in my bed

Its evil mantra trills in my brain

And pierces my heart over and over again

Can nothing or no one stop it?

This hideous, horrible refrain?

Or has it been the plan all along

To cause me to go insane?

Unhappy Forever

There is an empty space inside

It's so dark, nowhere to hide

Blackness, thick and closing in

It's hard to breathe, I feel it begin

Cloistering, sucking, the pulling weight

Shifting, swirling, filled with hate

Around me, inside me, I feel it fight

This empty feeling, black as night

I want the light, I call to it

It doesn't come for even a little bit

I can't stand up for I am so weak

My eyes full of liquid begin to leak

A flood of emotion so dark and benign

Washes over me making me blind

The tide of sorrow washes over me

And happiness again I'll never see

Choose To Break Free

The wall is high

Its strength unbreakable

The way seems impossible

To bust through and escape

There is no such thing

As a trap that cannot be escaped

Or a wall that cannot be scaled

Even when my eyes see it all that way

In those times

When it looks like despair closes in

And I am about to lose

And my heart all but faints within me

That is when You came

My rock, my fortress and my protector

You show me the way out

And I must choose to be brave enough to take it

This is me in a moment of breaking free.
During job training for my first full time job
after the divorce. The kids said I looked like
a new person and I felt like a new person
most of the time.

Magic Autumn

My skin prickled

Little hairs stood up on end

The wind whispered

And I shivered yet again

The damp earth around me

Covered with crisp, multicolored leaves

Rustled softly beneath

Each wispy wind sweep

I turned my face to the sun

Seeking some of its warmth

As another just came

And blew hair back from my face

Leaves blew up from the ground

Swirling in a tangled grace

I inhaled deeply of the crisp autumn air

Let it fill my lungs as it whipped my hair

In the midst of this glory

Of color, light and smell

And remembered whose magic

Created it all without spell

Evil Mantle

From North and South

From East and West

The wicked flood this way

In the glory of Summer

The dark of Winter

And the bright and flowering May

Like a magnet pulling

Iron filings in on itself

From this way and that

Wickedness and evil

The darkest and vile

On me their hatred spat

Covered in the dark and goo

And stained from all they have

Their heavy mantle about me sat

It's hard to stand

And bear the weight

Of what these forces wrought

It is hard to see

And hard to breathe

My head not clear for thought

The wicked all around me stand

Their gloating bright to see

Surreal and ugly, thick and odd

But a narrow light peaks through the dark

It hits something deep inside

Then I remember, a mighty fortress is my God

The fight is not mine

It matters not what I see or hear

He will lead me on the path my feet should lightly
trod

I am lifted up to stand again

But not with my own power

Remember? A mighty fortress is my God

Unrequited Love

Like a dull ache behind my eyes

Is the ache in my heart for you

A balloon bursts from too much pressure

As my heart does with love for you

Sometimes random images come to mind

And I lose my breath as I see you

Things happen in my life

And all I want is to share them with you

In my life there have been other loves

But none that I've loved like you

I can close my eyes and feel your touch

No one's touch has made me feel as you do

I see your eyes, your smile and hear your laugh in my mind

I know for me there is only you

And the ache and pain will never cease

Because you've turned away and I love you, still

Eagle

I had forgotten what it was like

The exhilaration of life

So long was I trapped down below

My soul filled with strife

The crushing darkness surrounding me

Fog thick enough to cut with a knife

Daylight into darkness, darkness into night

Never remembering myself, my true life

A ray of sunshine found me one day

And touched me in a special way

I felt the warmth and shook off the cold

And life began anew that day

I remembered myself and what I was before

I heard life beckon me to come play

My heart flew open to the flood of elation

And I knew life didn't have to be this way

I shook off the dust and gathered my strength

Preparing myself to take flight

I beat my wings with all my strength

Willing myself to gain height

The higher I went, the easier it became

My veiled eyes now open with full sight

I felt the wind beneath my wings

As I rise high above clouds in the night

A lovely eagle, mastering the skies and life

Filled with majesty, power and might

Frozen Art

In the cover of darkness

Amidst the cold, curling mist

It sits in waiting

Like a hard, tense fist

Frost spreads out beneath

And covers the hard, cool ground

The silence so crisp

In the absence of sound

Alone in the waiting

A crystallized work of art

Is the shivering remnant

Of what was once my heart

Unshed

There are tears inside

That I can't cry

And things I don't understand

No matter how I try

And feelings that I feel

But I can't explain why

The hope I've kept alive

I'm watching slowly die

Dreams and hopes sprout wings

And away they fly

Like the people in my life

I'm left to wave goodbye

So I sit with tears inside

That I can't cry

Wings

Hide me

Guard me

Under your fragrant wings of love

Love me

Shelter me

Under your soft wings of love

Speak to me

Keep me

Under your amazing wings of love

Nurture me

Guide me

Under your unchanging wings of love

Familiar

Here it comes again

That familiar feeling

That familiar pain

Wave after wave

Hits my body so hard

My heart, its slave

A simple sound

A simple smell

Drops me to the ground

My friend

My companion

This pain inside

I embrace it

Love it

Its lets me know I am alive

The Feeling of a Man

I miss the feel of a man

Holding me close

I miss the feel of a man

Dancing with me

I miss the feel of a man

Lying next to me

I miss the feel of a man

Kissing me

I miss the feel of a man

Touching me

I miss the feel of a man

Loving me

I miss the feel of a man

Looking at me

I miss the feel of a man

Protecting me

I miss the feel of a man

Holding my hand

I miss the feel of a man

Is it you?

My One

I want to feel that feeling

Of being looked at with love

The one that makes you feel special

And heat rise within

The one that makes you feel chosen

To know that you belong

I want to feel that feeling

Of being looked at with love

To know I inspire passion

Within my one

I want to be kissed like I matter

With tenderness and care

To feel depth and meaning

From my one

I'll know in an instant

When the time is right

Because I will feel that feeling

When I am looked at with love

And I'll be kissed like I matter

From the one, who is my one

Faith

Like the Cedars of Lebanon

Planted by the sea

With roots deeply planted

Defying gravity

Unshakable, unmoving

Let my faith be

Letting Go

Letting go of my past

Letting go of my fears

Letting go of the pain

Letting go of the tears

All of it was easy

Compared to letting go

Of you

I Choose

I choose sunshine, not rain

I choose laughter, instead of pain

I choose love, not hate

I choose my destiny, not fate

I choose happiness, not the sad

I choose to see good, instead of bad

I choose my life, not anyone else

I choose my life!

And to be in it, I choose you

Random

I am mostly random

random in my thoughts

random in my deeds

random how I dress

random what I eat

random what I read

random when I sleep

random in most everything

except when it comes to you

Angela Stevens & Me, Best Friends being random

Broken

I am broken

Broken on the inside

I am broken

All my tears cried

I am broken

My heart fried

I am broken

My patience tried

I am broken

I cannot hide

I am broken

Broken on the inside

Could've Been

It could've been you

That I saw in my dream

It could've been you

That I heard whisper in my ear

It could've been you

That held me close at night

It could've been you

On the journey that is my life

It could've been you

It could've been, what's beautiful and true

It could've been, but its not

But I still wish that it were you

Death Cup

Demons plague my soul

They haunt me day and night

Driving towards their ultimate goal

Wrenching from me all my fight

From the ground I look up

My body weak from the beating

I refuse the death cup

Never entertaining the thought of retreating

Like vultures picking apart their prey

Renting and tearing my flesh with their muzzle

Enjoying the carnage, the blood and decay

Their thirst drives them relentless to guzzle

Somewhere deep within me lies

A strength I never knew was there

It gathers strength as it does arise

Their greed will be their snare

I lift up my head, my will is strengthened

Light appears overhead and on my body shines

My life is restored and lengthened

And death no more has me with his spines

Dancing

In my mind I see it

The sky midnight blue

A breeze softly blowing

And me dancing with you

Music softly playing

Your cheek next to mine

Our bodies moving together

As the moonlight shines

In my mind I see it

In my heart I know its true

I long for that dance

As I long for you

Go

it should just go

all of what is bad

we should tell it to go

all that makes us sad

letting go should be easy

it should come without problems

but we grasp on to the very things

that should give us pause

letting go of my past

letting go of my fears

letting go of my pain

letting go of my tears

yes, it should be so easy

but we hold on to what we shouldn't

for me

letting go of everything else

wasn't as difficult as

letting go of you

Connection

My soul longs for a deep connection

One that goes beyond words

One that expresses deep affection

And causes my soul to fly with the wings of birds

Soul touching soul in a mysterious way

Timeless and formless but all the same real

Kindred spirits growing closer day by day

Causing wounds in each others' hearts to heal

My soul longs for that deep connection

One that defies expression

One that surpasses perfection

The one that causes my soul to freshen

God of my heart, you know what I need

What desires you place in me are for you to achieve

This thirst in my body and soul I can't cede

Help me to do what you've asked, to trust and believe

About the Author

Leslie Sowl lives in Ashland, Ohio with her three beautiful children and two ornery dogs. She has written devotionals for ministry magazines, contributed to martial arts books such as *Purpose Driven Martial Arts*, and she has written the manual used by her students at her martial arts school in Ashland, High Reaches Karate & Fitness, llc.

Leslie has a Bachelor's of Science in Education in addition to two second degree black belts in different disciplines. Leslie's primary discipline is Shinsei Hapkido and that is the focus of her attention when not with children or at work.

Find out more at www.HighReachesKarate.com